D0946479

WEEP NOT FOR ME

In Memory of a Beloved Cat

Constance Jenkins

Illustrated by Pat Schaverien

SOUVENIR PRESS

Weep not for me though I am gone
Into that gentle night.

Grieve if you will, but not for long,

Upon my soul's sweet flight.

I am at peace, my soul's at rest,

There is no need for tears;

For with your love I was so blessed

For all those many years.

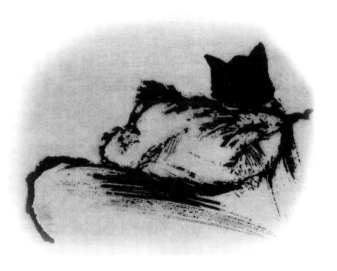

There is no pain, I suffer not;

The fear now all is gone.

Put now these things out of your thoughts,

In your memory I live on.

Remember not my fight for breath,

Remember not the strife.

Please do not dwell upon my death,
But celebrate my life.

In loving memory

of

Isolde

beloved companion

of Mary Jenkins

If you need someone to talk to about your loss...

<u>United Kingdom</u>
For information about the Pet Loss Befrienders
Service, contact either:
The Society for Companion Animal Studies
on 01877 330996
or:
The Blue Cross on 01993 822651

<u>United States</u>
Chicago Veterinary Medical Association/Delta
Society Pet Loss Helpline (708) 603-3994

University of Florida at Gainesville
Pet Loss Hotline (904) 338-2032

University of California at Davis
Pet Loss Help Line (916) 752-4200

The Delta Society (800) 869-6898

This edition first published 1999 by
Souvenir Press Ltd.,
43 Great Russell Street, London WC1B 3PA

ISBN 0 285 63492 5

Printed in Italy